495

Christ in You:
A Revelation of God's Power

by
Kim Wetteland

Harrison House, Inc.
Tulsa, Oklahoma

Unless otherwise indicated, all Scripture quotations are taken from the *King James Version* of the Bible.

Other quotations are from *The Amplified Bible, New Testament* (AMP). Copyright (c) 1954, 1958 by The Lockman Foundation, La Habra, California; or, from *The Amplified Bible, Old Testament* (AMP). Copyright (c) 1962, 1964 by Zondervan Publishing House, Grand Rapids, Michigan.

Christ in You:
A Revelation of God's Power
ISBN 0-89274-896-6
Copyright © 1992 by
Kim Wetteland
Kim Wetteland Ministries
P. O. Box 7652
Des Moines, IA 50322

Published by Harrison House, Inc.
P. O. Box 35035
Tulsa, OK 74153

Contents

Foreword

The new volume of Kim Wetteland's teaching called *Christ in You: A Revelation of God's Power*, is a message that is greatly needed. Nothing is more essential in our church world today, and in the total Body, as to be transformed into the image of Christ.

With much intercession of the Holy Spirit, the transformation work will be accomplished in the life of a believer. In presenting candid examples of this transformation, Pastor Wetteland in his book will assist the reader to understand the tremendous value in their personal lives of being transformed into the image of Christ.

As Pastor Wetteland describes in chapter 2, the transformation is not available to believers who do not have a keen desire to possess the image of Christ within.

In our present decade, with such an enormous need for spirituality and morality, seeking the image of Christ will result in divine conformity.

There is so much being written on so many topics today that a person has to choose what he has time to read. I am convinced that studying this book on *Christ in You: A Revelation of God's Power*, must have priority.

Dr. Lester Sumrall
South Bend, Indiana

1

In Need of Transformation

Some years ago, I participated in a field trip with my ninth grade junior high class. I will never forget my teacher, Mr. Teehay. Outwardly, he was a gruff man. Inwardly, he had a heart of pure gold. He dearly loved each student, treating each one as if he, or she, was his own son or daughter.

Ding! Ding! Ding! Ding! The school bell rang, and every student quickly found his seat. No messing around today! There was a field trip on the agenda. Each student quickly was accounted for as the room monitor took attendance.

"Does everyone have his lunch?" the monitor asked.

"Yeah!" came the unanimous cry from the students. As soon as everyone became quiet, Mr. Teehay gave his usual field-trip lecture on proper conduct. When he finished, everyone scurried for the bus.

What a great day! We were off to visit the shop of a wood carver. At this shop were all kinds of intricately cut pieces of wood. There were ornaments, animals, and figurines . . . everything you could imagine! A pleasant aroma of fresh-cut wood filled the air.

Then came the fun part. A distinguished-looking gentleman with greying hair and wire-rimmed glasses came out into the gallery from one of the back rooms. In his hand was a small piece of wood. There was nothing special about the wood. As a matter of fact, it was quite ordinary.

Before my very eyes, this distinguished-looking fellow picked up a little carving tool and began cutting away. Cut after cut after cut, and that ordinary piece of wood began to take on a new shape. After a half-hour of cutting, shaping, and etching, that ordinary piece of wood was transformed into a beautifully designed ornamental plaque.

Later, we found out this man was a master woodcarver. In a pair of ordinary hands, that small piece of wood might have been split into small pieces of kindling stock. Yet in the hands of the master woodcarver, a unique piece of creative art was born.

This is similar to the process that takes place when a person becomes a Christian. When we receive Jesus Christ as Lord and Savior, we are born again and become as that piece of wood in the Master Carver's hand.

> **For everyone who calls upon the name of the Lord** [invoking Him as Lord] **will be saved.**
> **Romans 10:13 AMP**

When we become born again, Satan can no longer manipulate, rule, and dominate our lives. We are changed! God becomes our Father. We are translated out of the kingdom of darkness into the Kingdom of Light. We take the seat of royalty with Jesus Christ in heavenly places. Our spirits are born again.

> . . . **Unless a person is born again** (anew, from above), **he cannot ever see** (know, be acquainted with, and experience) **the kingdom of God.**
> **John 3:3 AMP**

> . . . **And I pray God your whole** *spirit* **and** *soul* **and** *body* **be preserved blameless unto the coming of our Lord Jesus Christ.**
> **1 Thessalonians 5:23**

In this verse, the Apostle Paul clearly indicates that man is a three-part being: spirit, soul, and body. We *are* a spirit. We *have* a soul, made up of mind, or intellect, will, and emotions. And we *live* in a physical body.

Our bodies have not been born again. Christians still age, just as unsaved human beings, and experience physical death.

> **. . . It is appointed unto men once to die, but after this the judgment.**
>
> **Hebrews 9:27**

Neither are our souls born again. Our minds, wills, and emotions must continually be renewed by God's Word. Only our spirits are changed, recreated as brand new babies, when we receive Christ's lordship over our lives. Your spirit is the *real you.*

This is where we must make a distinction. As a Christian, your spirit has been created again. You are a brand new creation in Christ.

> **Therefore if any man be in Christ, he is a new creature: old things are passed away; behold, all things are become new.**
>
> **2 Corinthians 5:17**

To be born again, however, does not mean you immediately become like Jesus. Being fashioned into the exact image and likeness of Jesus is a process that happens day by day as we faithfully spend time in worship, prayer, and the study of God's Word.

> **. . . but though our outward man perish, yet the inward man is renewed day by day.**
>
> **2 Corinthians 4:16**

As we spend time intimately communing with Jesus, our flesh is crucified and our born-again, newly created spirit becomes fashioned into the glorious image of Christ.

While on the field trip I mentioned, I watched a master woodcarver transform an ordinary piece of wood into a beautifully designed work of art. The piece of wood was in need of a transformation. As born-again Christians, we, too, are in need of a transformation. God's will is that each one of us fully take on the exact image and likeness of our Lord and Savior, Jesus Christ.

For whom he did foreknow, he also did predestinate *to be conformed to the image of his son* . . . .

Romans 8:29

2

There Must Be a Desire To Change

But if our gospel be hid, it is hid to them that are lost:

In whom the god of this world hath blinded the minds of them which believe not, lest the light of the glorious gospel of Christ, *who is the image of God,* should shine unto them.

2 Corinthians 4:3,4

Jesus Christ is the exact image of God the Father. The Greek word for *image* is *eikon,* which also means "likeness, resemblance, or exact representation." He is God manifest in the flesh to this lost and dying world.

Jesus said, . . . **He that hath seen me hath seen the Father** . . . (John 14:9).

The Greek word for *seen* is *horao,* which means "to clearly discern, perceive, and comprehend." Can you grasp what Christ is saying? It actually is possible to have a clear discernment, perception, and comprehension of God's Son! As we receive a glimpse of Christ, a transformation process begins. We are becoming like Jesus.

Beloved, now are we the sons of God, and it doth not yet appear what we shall be: but we know that, when he shall appear, we shall be like him; for we shall see him as he is.

1 John 3:2

As we are transformed into the exact likeness of Jesus, the process towards full comprehension of Him begins. Yet, how could this be? Although this is a great mystery, it is very simple. The deep things of God always are simple —

11

simple to the spirit, and yet, unsearchable to the natural mind.

To survive in today's society, we must learn to walk and live in the spirit. Living in the realm of the Holy Spirit is not an option! The day of having God's Word in our heads with our inward beings left untouched is over.

Jesus Christ is the incarnation of God's eternal Word. In like manner, we also must become the personification of Christ to those we know and meet. Our spirits must fully be transformed into His exact image, likeness, and resemblance. It is through this process of change that we begin to comprehend Christ. Why? It is because whatever we become inwardly, we naturally perceive and comprehend. Transformation always brings enlightenment.

Jesus Christ is God. As we grow in our perception of Him, we literally are beginning to comprehend portions of God's vastness.

Many theologians claim there is no possibility of comprehending God at this level. Yet the Bible declares that we, *with all the saints*, will comprehend the breadth, length, depth, and height — in other words, fully discern — Christ's love which surpasses natural understanding.

> **For this cause I bow my knees unto the Father of our Lord Jesus Christ.**
>
> **Of whom the whole family in heaven and earth is named.**
>
> **That he would grant you, according to the riches of his glory, to be strengthened with might by his Spirit in the inner man;**
>
> **That Christ may dwell in your hearts by faith; that ye, being rooted and grounded in love,**
>
> **May be able to *comprehend with all saints* what is the breadth, and length, and depth, and height;**

And to know the love of Christ, which passeth knowledge, that ye might be filled with all the fulness of God.

Ephesians 3:14-18

A price must be paid to comprehend God at this level. We must be willing to change. We must be willing to patiently stay in God's holy presence until the flesh is crucified, and we experience a transformation — until we experience Christ.

I am crucified with Christ: nevertheless I live; yet not I, but Christ liveth in me: and the life which I now live in the flesh I live by the faith of the Son of God, who loved me, and gave himself for me.

Galatians 2:20

The Christian of today's decade will thrive on change, and as a result, will walk in great supernatural power and authority. Power over disease, demons, and even nature. As the winds and the seas obeyed Christ, they will also obey those who would dare to allow a complete transformation into Christ's image to take place in their hearts.

And I, brethren, when I came to you, came not with excellency of speech or of wisdom, declaring unto you the testimony of God.

For I determined not to know any thing among you, save Jesus Christ, and him crucified.

And I was with you in weakness, and in fear, and in much trembling.

And *my speech* and *my preaching* was not with enticing words of man's wisdom, but in *demonstration* of the Spirit and power.

1 Corinthians 2:1-4

Paul was a man who walked in great power and authority. When he spoke, miracles occurred. There was power in Paul's words, in his preaching as well as in his common, ordinary, everyday speech.

When Paul spoke God's eternal, written Word, power thundered forth from his inward man. The intriguing thing about Paul, however, is that this same miraculous occurrence took place when he spoke his own words.

The book of Galatians records that Paul spent three years in Arabia and Damascus, communing with Christ through worship, prayer, and studying God's Word. Paul paid a price to walk in the kind of power he displayed. He stayed in God's presence until Christ completely was revealed in his spirit.

> **But I certify you, brethren, that the gospel which was preached of me is not after man.**
>
> **For I neither received it of man, neither was I taught it, but by the revelation of Jesus Christ.**
>
> **For ye have heard of my conversation in time past in the Jews' religion, how that beyond measure I persecuted the church of God, and wasted it:**
>
> **And profited in the Jews' religion above many my equals in mine own nation, being more exceedingly zealous of the traditions of my fathers.**
>
> **But when it pleased God, who separated me from my mother's womb, and called me by his grace,**
>
> *To reveal his Son in me,* **that I might preach him among the heathen; immediately I conferred not with flesh and blood.**
>
> **Galatians 1:11-16**

Paul could instruct us to pray without ceasing, because he knew what it was to pray without ceasing. (1 Thess. 5:17.)

Paul could say, "For me to live is Christ and to die is gain" (Phil. 1:21), because he stayed in God's presence long enough for his flesh to be crucified and his inward man to be fashioned into the glorious image of Jesus Christ.

Paul had authority, because he afforded God the time to fashion his spirit into the exact likeness, resemblance, and representation of the Living Word Himself — Jesus! He exuded great power because his words were spoken out of a life that had undergone transformation.

Paul became like Jesus on the inside. As a result, his words expressed great power and authority on the outside. He could have read a cookbook out loud, and great power still would have been released! Why? That was because he spoke out of a life that had undergone change.

Keep thy heart with all diligence; for out of it are the issues of life.

Proverbs 4:23

Paul kept his heart diligently in the presence of Jesus so he could become like Jesus. As Christ was imaged in Paul's heart, the issues of *life, power, and authority* flowed freely from his spirit as he spoke. His words carried a tangible manifestation of the Holy Spirit's presence and power.

God's will is that every Christian be conformed to the image of Christ.

For whom he did foreknow, he also did predestinate to be conformed to the image of his Son . . . .

Romans 8:29

As we allow God to fashion our spiritmen into His likeness, we will walk in Christ's power. The same power Paul had in his life, we can have, too. But we must be willing to experience change. Confessing God's Word without a changed life will not work.

As mentioned earlier, *image* in the Greek is *eikon,* which means "an exact image."

In other words, Paul wrote: "Those whom He foreknew, He ordained to be conformed to the *exact* image and likeness of His Son."

The word *conformed* in the Greek is *summorphos,* which means "jointly formed." We could read Romans 8:29 as follows:

"For those He did foreknow, He also did predestinate to be jointly formed into the exact image and likeness of His son, Jesus Christ."

We must live in intimacy with Jesus, giving the Holy Spirit free reign to form the jewels of Christ inside of us, transforming us into His exact representation and image.

This transformation takes place in a joint relationship with Jesus Christ. Without Christ, we can do nothing.

I am the vine, ye are the branches: He that abideth in me, and I in him, the same bringeth forth much fruit: for without me ye can do nothing.

John 15:5

We cannot conform *ourselves* into His image. It is a joint effort. Our part of that effort means coming into His presence and yielding to Him. His effort is to work in our inner beings by the Holy Spirit to conform us into His glorious image.

As we become like Jesus on the inside, our words will carry great power and lasting authority on the outside. As I stated earlier, confessing God's Word without yielding to the Holy Spirit's transforming grace, will not work.

3
Two Kinds of Authority

As Christians, we have authority over demons, disease, and disasters through speaking God's Word and using the name of Jesus. This is one kind of authority.

There is, however, another kind of authority which comes as a result of a continual, ongoing, inward transformation. A price must be paid to receive this kind of authority. As I stated at the close of chapter 2, as we become conformed to the image of Jesus on the inside, our words carry great power and lasting authority on the outside.

I am thankful that God has given us the privilege of using the name of Jesus and speaking His Word. There is power in the name of Jesus. There is power through speaking the written Word of God. I am thankful for that. But there is another level of authority available to any Christian who will dare to undergo the process of being transformed into the glorious image of Jesus Christ.

This is a level of authority where common, ordinary, everyday speech carries and releases a tangible manifestation of the Holy Spirit's presence and power. For as we are transformed into the exact likeness, image, and resemblance of Jesus on the inside, our *own* words carry great power and lasting authority on the outside.

> **And these attesting signs will accompany those who believe: in My name they will drive out demons: they will speak in new languages;**

> **They will pick up serpents, and** [even] **if they drink anything deadly, it will not hurt them; they will lay their hands on the sick, and they will get well.**
> **Mark 16:17,18 AMP**

As Christians, we have the right and authority to use the name of Jesus. Demons, disease, and disasters are subject to us through the mighty name of Jesus.

Authority in the Name of Jesus

When I was a teenager, my mother had severe migraine headaches. It was not unusual for her to be in bed for seven days with a migraine. She would have a headache so bad at times that Dad would drive her to the emergency room at the local hospital. Each time, her doctor would prescribe a series of three different shots: one to stop the vomiting, one to deaden the pain, and one to knock her out so she could sleep.

On one occasion, Mom spent three weeks in bed with absolutely no relief. She was a real fighter, but no matter how hard she fought, she was unable to find enough strength to ward off this horrid satanic grip. She needed authority from Someone of a Higher Power.

One day, Mom was in the kitchen washing dishes. It was a bright, sunny July day. It was the first day she had been up and able to do anything for quite some time. The migraine finally had subsided after ten days in bed. I picked up a towel and helped her by drying the dishes. We laughed as we shared good times.

In the course of our conversation, I asked her if she believed Jesus had given her power and authority over migraine headaches.

"Well, of course I believe that Jesus has given me power and authority over migraine headaches! His word says so," she exclaimed.

18

If there is a person on earth who knows the Word of God, it is my mother. After she received the baptism in the Holy Spirit with evidence of speaking in other tongues, she read God's Word from sunup until sundown. If she was not reading the Bible, she was listening to Kenneth Copeland's teaching tapes.

Mom's problem was not a lack of knowing God's Word. She knew the Bible backwards and forwards. Her problem was a failure to apply the Word of God in her life by *doing* it.

> **But be doers of the Word [obey the message], and not merely listeners to it, betraying yourselves** [into deception by reasoning contrary to the Truth].
> **James 1:22 AMP**

Many Christians today have the same problem. They know what the Bible says, and yet, they fail to apply God's Word to their lives by doing what it says.

After talking with Mom for quite some time, I said, "Mom, if you believe Jesus gave you power and authority over migraine headaches, how long are you going to allow the devil to keep giving them to you? Are you hanging onto them so other people will feel sorry for you, or what?"

With some folks, you have to say things that will shock them into realizing that they are not doing the things they think they are doing. On numerous occasions, Jesus did this, also. Mom truly believed that she was applying the Word of God to her life. However, like most Christians, she became lax and was not applying God's Word to her life by *doing* what it said.

When we fail to do what God's Word tells us to do, we fall into the deception of thinking that our agreement with the Word is enough to put us over. To merely agree with the fact that the Bible is true, and yet fail to have our speech and actions line up with it, is not true faith.

So also faith, if it does not have works (deeds and actions of obedience to back it up), **by itself is destitute of power** (inoperative, dead).

James 2:17 AMP

A few days after our conversation in the kitchen, Mom and Dad were driving to one of their favorite restaurants to have breakfast. As they drove along, Mom started to get another severe headache, just like the ones she had experienced so many times in the past. Mom knew the Bible was true. She believed with her whole heart that Jesus had given her power and authority over migraine headaches.

And the seventy returned again with joy, saying, Lord, even the devils are subject unto us through thy name.

And he said unto them, I beheld Satan as lightning fall from heaven.

Behold, I give unto you power to tread on serpents and scorpions, and over all the power of the enemy: and nothing shall by any means hurt you.

Luke 10:17-19

As the pain intensified, Mom began to think of the conversation she had with me several days earlier.

She began to hear my question to her over and over: "If you believe Jesus gave you power and authority over migraine headaches, how long are you going to allow the devil to keep giving them to you?"

Finally, James 4:7 popped into her mind!

So be subject to God. Resist the devil [stand firm against him] **and he will flee from you.**

James 4:7 AMP

"Stop the car!" Mom yelled at Dad.

Then, with authority and boldness, she began to shout, "You foul migraine headache. In the name of Jesus, you get out of my head, and don't you ever come back again!"

Dad pulled back onto the road and proceeded to the restaurant. Halfway through breakfast, Mom realized the headache had gone. For years, she had agreed with God's Word and sincerely believed it was true. Yet she had done nothing to enforce Satan's defeat. Agreeing that the Bible is true without doing anything to resist Satan will not force him to flee. We must resist the sickness, fear, or tormenting thought in the name of Jesus. Then, they will go.

When Mom agreed with God's Word and did nothing, the headaches recurred. But when she forcefully commanded the migraine to leave in the name of Jesus, it left. Since that incident fifteen years ago, she has not had one migraine headache. There is power in the name of Jesus.

Several years before entering into fulltime ministry, I was serving as an usher at a church in Tulsa, Oklahoma. It was the Sunday evening service. The pastor was preaching a powerful message when, suddenly, a man leaped onto the platform and began to slither around on his belly like a snake.

A number of ushers, including myself, converged on the man from all directions. He was hissing and spitting, and his tongue, which protruded four inches in length from out his mouth, was forked exactly like the tongue of a rattlesnake.

Although we had heard of similar incidents occurring in Africa, Haiti, and South America, we had never seen anything like this with our own eyes. The man was physically removed from the platform and taken to a room away from the main service.

As long as I live, I never will forget what happened after the door of that room was closed. With the piercing eyes of a snake, the man looked straight at me, put his hands around my throat, and said, "I'm going to kill you!"

As startled as I was, something rose up on the inside of me, deep within my spirit, something strong, mighty, and militant.

But when they deliver you up, take no thought how or what ye shall speak: for it shall be given you in that same hour what ye shall speak.

For it is not ye that speak, but the Spirit of your Father which speaketh in you.

Matthew 10:19,20

With great boldness, I looked straight into the eyes of that demon-possessed man. With his hands still firmly gripping my throat, I said, "Who am I?"

I have learned the value of leaning on the Holy Spirit when dealing with demonic principalities and powers. The Holy Spirit will give you the right words to speak, no matter how critical the situation. Never in my entire life would I have remotely imagined that the right response to a demon-possessed man clutching my throat would be to ask the simple question, "Who am I?"

In a deep, quivering voice, the demon spoke directly through the man, saying, "You are a servant of the Most High God, and Jesus Christ is the One whom you serve."

"That's right," I said, "And in His name, you come out of this man. Loose him right now!"

Before my eyes, the man rose completely off the floor, levitated to a position about four feet in the air, and came crashing down with many demons screaming as they left, one by one. The man was completely and instantly delivered.

Today, he is happily married with four children and travels throughout the country teaching and preaching the same Gospel message that set him free. There is power in the name of Jesus.

Demand Results in Christ's Name

And whatsoever ye shall ask in my name, that will I do, that the Father may be glorified in the Son.

If ye shall ask any thing in my name, I will do it.
John 14:13,14

In this scripture, the Greek word for *ask* is *aiteo*, which means "to ask, require, or demand." Jesus tells us that we are allowed to put great demands upon His name. In fact, Jesus said that if we demand anything in His name, He will do it.

This is where many Christians become confused and try to order God around as if He were a puppet. This, however, is not what Christ was instructing us to do. We cannot demand that God do anything. But we can demand that Satan, his demons, disease, and disasters back off and move away in the mighty name of Jesus. In fact, the Scripture commands every Christian to do this.

And the Lord said, If ye had faith as a grain of mustard seed, ye might say unto this sycamine tree, Be thou plucked up by the root, and be thou planted in the sea; and it should obey you.
Luke 17:8

We must become bold and insist that Satan release his grip off the lives of hurting people. We must demand sickness and every kind of disease to flee in the name of Jesus. As we do, Jesus will see to it that our words are carried out as spoken. Every Christian has the legal right and authority to use the name of Jesus and to back off the powers of hell.

In what traditionally is known as The Lord's Prayer (Mt. 6:9-13), Jesus said we are to pray like this:

After this manner therefore pray ye: Our Father which art in heaven, Hallowed be thy name.

Thy kingdom come. Thy will be done in earth, as it is in heaven.

Matthew 6:9,10

This does not mean we are simply to mumble some "namby, pamby" kind of prayer, pleading with God to carry out His will on earth because we are so weak, beaten down, and miserable. On the contrary, we must yield to God's strength and become militant. We must sit in the presence of Christ until we are filled with great boldness.

Then as we pray for the sick, the oppressed, and the afflicted in the name of Jesus, we must demand that every bondage be broken in order for the will of God to be done on earth just as it is in heaven.

God's will is that every sick person be healed. God's will is that every oppressed person be set free. Every Christian has the responsibility to use the name of Jesus, crush the powers of hell, and demonstrate the will of God on earth as it is in heaven.

We are not to merely pray *for* the will of God to be done. No! We are to pray in such a way that His will *is* done. To pray in this fashion means that we must use the name of Jesus with great boldness against anything that would harm or injure mankind. This is one kind of authority: the authority, right, and responsibility of using the name of Jesus.

4

Authority in Your Own Words

There is another kind of authority available to all who dare to persist in experiencing a complete transformation of the inward man into the glorious image of Jesus Christ. A price must be paid to walk in this type of authority.

> And it came to pass, as we went to prayer, a certain damsel possessed with a spirit of divination met us, which brought her masters much gain by soothsaying:
>
> The same followed Paul and us, and cried, saying, These men are the servants of the most high God, which shew unto us the way of salvation.
>
> And this did she many days. But Paul, being grieved, turned and said to the spirit, I command thee in the name of Jesus Christ to come out of her. And he came out the same hour.
>
> Acts 16:16-18

In this scripture, we see an example of the Apostle Paul's use of the name of Jesus with boldness and authority to cast a demon spirit of divination out of a woman. This is the kind of authority I discussed in the last chapter: the right to use the name of Jesus to exercise authority over demons, disease, and disasters.

> And God wrought special miracles by the hands of Paul:
>
> So that from his body were brought unto the sick handkerchiefs or aprons, and the diseases departed from them, and the evil spirits went out of them.
>
> Acts 19:11,12

In Acts 19, we see a different kind of authority in action. We do not see Paul taking authority through the name of Jesus as he did with the demon-possessed woman in Acts 16. Instead, we simply see handerkerchiefs and aprons from his body being laid upon the sick and demon-oppressed. The same results occurred as when he had used the name of Jesus: Diseases departed, and evil spirits went out!

These miracles were called *special,* because they only occur in this fashion when an individual begins to experience a genuine transformation of his inward man into the *exact* likeness and image of Jesus Christ by yielding to the Holy Spirit's deeper works of purging grace.

By and large, the Church has failed to demonstrate great and unusual expressions of power, because it has been unwilling to change. We have wanted to speak God's Word, make our ''faith confessions,'' and still live in the flesh.

I have seen many Christians pray over small pieces of cloth and place them on sick folks with some degree of results. I have done this myself. But few are those who can simply take their shirts off, lay them upon individuals who are near death, and see deliverance occur instantaneously.

Yet this is exactly what Paul did. Handkerchiefs and aprons were part of the normal everyday wardrobe for a Jew in Paul's day. Paul simply removed pieces of his common clothing and gave them to others to lay upon those who were sick and demon-oppressed. The results were immediate and always supernatural.

When items of clothing were taken from Paul's body to be laid upon others, he said nothing. Paul did not pray, groan, shout, release God's anointing into his clothes, or do any of that stuff. He did not have to! Please do not misunderstand — I am not poking fun at those who do such things. I just want you to realize there is a *higher* level of authority available to those who dare to pay the price to walk in it.

> **But when it pleased God, who separated me from my mother's womb, and called me by his grace,**
>
> **To reveal his Son in me, that I might preach him among the heathen; immediately I conferred not with flesh and blood:**
>
> **Neither went I up to Jerusalem to them which were apostles before me; but I went into Arabia, and returned again unto Damascus.**
>
> **Galatians 1:15-17**

What did Paul do during the years he spent in Arabia and Damascus? During every moment of those three precious years, Paul *diligently* sought the heart of God and stayed in His presence until Jesus Christ was formed within his inward man. He committed himself to worship, prayer, the study of God's Word, and yielding to the Holy Spirit's deeper works of purging grace. Paul experienced a change, because he diligently sought for it.

Paul became so much like Jesus on the inside that his clothes (on the outside) naturally carried God's anointing. Paul did not have to pray over his clothes to release the anointing of God into them. Carrying the anointing of God in his clothing was a natural consequence of the life Paul lived in union with Christ.

As we join ourselves to Jesus, we become one spirit with Him. (1 Cor. 5:17.) To become one spirit with Christ is to experience a complete transformation of the inward man, the highest level of authority a Christian can obtain. At this level of authority, anything you do or say releases a tangible manifestation of the Holy Spirit's presence with great power following.

Every Christian may experience a measure of authority through speaking God's Word and using the name of Jesus. Every Christian, however, will not experience the release of great power when his *own* words are spoken. A price must be paid to walk in this kind of authority. It is called "the price of dying to self."

And my speech and my preaching was not with enticing words of man's wisdom, but in demonstration of the Spirit and of power.

1 Corinthians 2:4

A closer look at this scripture will reveal that a great manifestation of the Holy Spirit's presence and power were released when Paul preached God's Word. An even closer examination reveals that this same release of power and authority occurred when Paul spoke his own words. Paul's common, ordinary, everyday speech expressed the same tangible manifestation of power as his preaching.

Paul's Words Had Life-Changing Power

As Paul sold his tents in the marketplace, he conversed with the citizens in the common, "street" version of the Greek language of the day. Small talk and the daily routines of life were part of the normal business conversation for the average Jew. But when Paul spoke, something was different. It was not so much the words that he spoke as it was the life-changing power behind those words.

A sense of conviction with eternal consequences was clearly conveyed, whether Paul spoke God's Word or his own word. Power always was released! Why did this happen? As we become conformed into the image and likeness of Jesus on the inside, our own words carry great power and lasting authority on the outside.

We see this same kind of dominion released in the life of Jesus shortly before His crucifixion.

And he came out, and went, as he was wont, to the mount of Olives; and his disciples also followed him.

And when he was at the place, he said unto them, Pray that ye enter not into temptation.

And he was withdrawn from them about a stone's
cast, and kneeled down, and prayed,

Saying, Father, if thou be willing, remove this cup
from me: nevertheless not my will, but thine, be done.

And there appeared an angel unto him from heaven,
strengthening him.

And being in an agony he prayed more earnestly: and
his sweat was as it were great drops of blood falling down
to the ground.

And when he rose up from prayer, and was come to
his disciples, he found them sleeping for sorrow,

And said unto them, Why sleep ye? rise and pray,
lest ye enter into temptation.

Luke 22:39-46

In becoming human, Jesus humbled Himself and laid
down His divine rights and privileges.

Let this same attitude and purpose and [humble]
mind be in you which was in Christ Jesus: [Let Him
be your example in humility:]

Who, although being essentially one with God
and in the form of God [possessing the fullness of the
attributes which make God God], did not think this
equality with God was a thing to be eagerly grasped
or retained.

But stripped Himself [of all privileges and rightful
dignity], so as to assume the guise of a servant (slave),
in that He became like men and was born a human
being.

Philippians 2:5-7 AMP

Sometimes I wonder if many of us have a Holy Spirit-
inspired revelation of how human Jesus really was. The fact
is Jesus became so fully human that He had a human will
which He had to resist, just like you and me. This is depicted
clearly in the struggle Jesus faced in the Garden of
Gethsemane.

The greatest struggle of temptation Jesus faced was not against the devil, but against His own *human* will. Again, please do not misunderstand. The Bible says that Jesus had His face set "as a flint" to go to the cross for everyone. (Isa. 50:7.) Yet, because He was human as well as divine, Jesus had to resist temptation as forcefully as any of us. Yet He was tempted *without sin*.

> **For we have not an high priest which cannot be touched with the feeling of our infirmities; but was in all points tempted like as we are, yet without sin.**
> **Hebrews 4:15**

As He prayed, there was a struggle. The flesh never gives up easily. Christ began to agonize and sweat as it were great drops of blood. His words echoed with the force of great commitment: **. . . nevertheless not my will, but thine, be done** (Luke 22:42). The final results were never in question. Walking in the Spirit will break the resistance of human flesh every time.

People have strange ideas sometimes in regard to being "broken." Many believe falsely that God sends sickness, torment, and tragedy to break hardened wills. No! Being broken is a decision. God will not break someone against his free will and choice.

You must choose to intimately commune with God daily so the presence of His Holy Spirit can break the power of your human flesh. Being broken can occur only as you come into intimacy with Jesus through consistent yielding to the Holy Spirit's deep, inner purgings. The flesh — a hindrance to God's will being accomplished in your life — then is crucified and stripped away from the spirit.

It is hard on the flesh to sit in the presence of God each day. That is why many simply will not do it. In the presence of the living Spirit, the flesh finds its end. The pride of life has no place. Plans, purposes, and pursuits which have been centered around a "life of self" must go.

Unfortunately, for some, this is too much to ask. This is why the Church has failed to demonstrate great power.

A price must be paid to walk in the kind of authority where our own words carry a tangible manifestation of the Holy Spirit's power. We have wanted to speak the Word, make faith confessions, use the name of Jesus, and pamper the flesh at the same time. It cannot be done. That type of lukewarm passivity will not hold up today.

Although Jesus was fully God manifest in the flesh, He made sure His human, fleshly will did not dictate His destiny. There never was a doubt about the final outcome. As I shared earlier, walking in the Spirit always will break the resistance of human flesh.

Flesh Cannot Resist the Spirit

As Christ made His exit from the Garden of Gethsemane, He was met by Judas Iscariot and a band of men from the temple.

> So Judas, obtaining and taking charge of the band of soldiers and some guards (attendants) of the high priests and Pharisees, came there with lanterns and torches and weapons.
>
> Then Jesus, knowing all that was about to befall Him, went out to them and said, Whom are you seeking? [Whom do you want?]
>
> They answered Him, Jesus the Nazarene. Jesus said to them, I am He. Judas, who was betraying Him, was also standing with them.
>
> When Jesus said to them, I am He, they went backwards (drew back, lurched backward) and fell to the ground.
>
> John 18:3-6 AMP

I want you to notice something here. Something common, ordinary, and, yet, extremely powerful. As these men were approaching, Jesus knew the fate which would befall Him.

"Who are you looking for?" Jesus asked boldly, and the reply came, "Jesus, the Nazarene." Then came the response: "I am He."

There was nothing fancy, super-spiritual, or unique about Christ's answer. He simply admitted who He was, an average, common, ordinary answer, but one which had a uniquely unusual, supernatural response. The men fell backwards to the ground, so great was the release of power from His ordinary statement.

There is power through speaking and confessing the Word of God. There also is power in using the name of Jesus. But for those who will dare to resist their own fleshly wills to the point that nothing is left in them but Christ, there is power and authority in common, average, ordinary words.

As we are fashioned into the exact likeness and image of Jesus on the inside, our own words will carry great power and lasting authority on the outside. Those who are willing to fully "die out to self" will carry the greatest anointing in the days that lie ahead.

I remember one such individual who influenced my life greatly. That was a dear saint named Jeannie Wilkerson. "Sister Wilkerson" was known to spend long periods of time in daily fellowship with the heavenly Father. When she spoke, great power was released, and the lives of people always were changed.

One encounter I had with Mrs. Wilkerson transformed my life forever, and I will always remember it. It was a Wednesday evening, and I was parking my car at church. I happened to pull up next to her as she also was parking. While walking to the building, I offered her a hand of assistance.

A very gracious woman, Mrs. Wilkerson responded by saying, "Why, thank you. I appreciate that."

As she spoke, Jesus oozed out of her spirit like butter and honey. Nothing like that had ever happened to me before. She did not pray for me, touch me, or even speak the name of Jesus. She simply thanked me. Yet when she spoke, there was power!

God's holy presence came all over me. I was overwhelmed with a sense of reverence for the most Holy One and fell out under the power, right there in the parking lot. Some folks call that "being slain in the Spirit."

Then, she began to prophesy, and you have not heard prophecy until you have heard her! (Mrs. Wilkerson now has gone to be with the Lord.) To receive a prophetic utterance from her was like being pierced with arrows of love and correction at the same time. She did not give "bless-me" prophecies to pet the flesh. She would bathe you in God's presence until you met Christ in a new way. When she spoke, there was power!

I never was the same after that incident. I had met God in a new way and forever was changed. Mrs. Wilkerson paid a price to walk in that kind of power. She had no regard or respect for the flesh at all. She was known to spend hours in prayer every day. She emptied herself until there was nothing left but Christ. She became so much like Jesus on the inside that anything she spoke demonstrated great authority and power on the outside. This is the kind of power the Church needs today. But a price must be paid to receive it.

Once, I was conducting a Wednesday-evening service at The Lighthouse Christian Center in Richmond, Virginia. What a service that was! I shared a powerful message from the Lord and many people came for prayer. God moved powerfully, and miraculous healings took place. One in particular, I recall with great vividness. A woman with double vision remained in her seat and did not come forward. For seven years, she had been to many physicians, taken various medications, and undergone surgeries. Her vision had not improved.

When I approached her, I knew in my spirit that something mighty was going to happen. With the entire congregation looking on, I prayed — and nothing happened! Deep in my inner man, the Spirit of God was speaking to me, saying, "Spit in her eyes."

"There is no way I can do that," I reasoned. "Everyone will think I am crazy."

After several uneventful attempts at doing things my way, I finally decided to obey God, and so I spit in the woman's eyes. As I did so, she jumped to her feet and began to scream.

"Glory to God, I can see clearly!" she shouted.

At that point, all heaven broke loose, and the glory fell. Everyone in the church knew of this woman's eye problems. This was a miracle that sparked a fire in the hearts of everyone there.

While praying for several other individuals on the platform, I saw a man dressed in a ragged blue-jean jacket slowly moving toward the front. Something was not right. I knew immediately in my spirit that the man was demon-possessed. As my eyes focused directly on his eyes, he began to hiss, growl, and utter non-sensible words.

Then, with an authority that hardly can be put in descriptive terms, I jumped off the platform, grabbed the man by the shoulders, and shouted, "Come out right now! You unclean spirit! Loose him!"

The man instantly was delivered and in his right mind, but for a long time this disturbed me. That was the first time I ever commanded a demon to come out of a man without using the name of Jesus. I did not even know why I did not. All I did was sense the power of the Holy Spirit and flow with Him. A spiritual confrontation occurred, I became aware of it, told the demon to leave, and it did.

However, please do not "build a doctrine" off my experience and stop using the name of Jesus. Use His name always. Simply understand that greater anointings are available to those who will yield to the deeper purgings of the Holy Spirit's work.

> **And it shall come to pass in that day, that his burden shall be taken away from off thy shoulder, and his yoke from off thy neck, and the yoke shall be destroyed because of the anointing.**
>
> **Isaiah 10:27**

Confession Must Be From the Spirit

I am thankful for the tremendous faith ministries that have arisen in the Church over the past 30 years. Without faith, it is impossible to please God. (Heb. 11:6.) Yet I am concerned that we have learned faith so well that many imitate faith with flesh.

When an individual begins to fully "die out to self" and experience a true crucifixion of the flesh, *any word spoken becomes an anointed word.* I am not against "confessing God's Word." In fact, I am all for it; however, when we "confess God's Word" by asserting the flesh, we have not broken free from our fleshly wills. To speak God's Word with flesh is still flesh! There is no release of power.

> **Death and life are in the power of the tongue: and they that love it shall eat the fruit thereof.**
>
> **Proverbs 18:21**

This scripture tells us that death *and* life are in the power of the tongue. If we confess God's Word through the power of our flesh, the only power released is fleshly power. Fleshly power will not destroy yokes of hellish bondage. This is the reason we have some Christians who religiously "confess God's Word" with little or no results. We first must "die to self" for the power of the Spirit to be resting upon the things we say.

We may speak God's Word with great boldness, but until our flesh is dealt with, flesh will still be the true source of power behind our confession of God's Word. When flesh speaks God's Word, there is no release of power, no tangible manifestation of the Holy Spirit's presence that destroys the yoke; thus, no results.

This, however, is *not* the message the Church wants to hear. We want to make "faith confessions," use the name of Jesus, and still live in the flesh. Jesus said we must take up our cross and follow Him. (Mt. 16:24.) To survive in these days, our commitments must grow. The number-one priority must be to practice living in the presence of the Holy Spirit, where flesh and self will find an end.

For if ye live after the flesh, ye shall die: but if ye through the Spirit do mortify the deeds of the body, ye shall live.

Romans 8:13

Flesh becomes crucified through basking in the glory. This is how we "die out to self:" through intimate communion with Christ, through living a life of worship, prayer, and time spent in the scriptures. As the flesh and self-will are crucified, there is only one source left to empower our words: **Christ in you, the hope of glory** (Col. 1:27).

When Christ alone remains with the fullness of His image etched on our inward beings, anything we say will carry a tangible manifestation of the Spirit's presence that destroys the yoke. Sickness will have no choice but to flee in submission to our commands. Demons must obey our declarations. Principalities must forfeit their control over our churches, cities, and nations.

I am thankful for the power in God's Word. I am eternally grateful for the authority God has made available to every Christian through the name of Jesus. But I want *everything* God has made available to us. I want what Paul the Apostle experienced!

> **And my speech (common, ordinary words) and my preaching was not with enticing words of man's wisdom, but in demonstration of the Spirit and of power.**
>
> **1 Corinthians 2:4**

I want my common, ordinary, everyday conversation to release a tangible manifestation of the Holy Spirit's presence that destroys every yoke. When Jeannie Wilkerson spoke to me in the parking lot, there was nothing special about her words. It was the anointing that was special, the presence of the Holy Spirit. She paid a price to receive it. She sacrificed her own will and "died out to self."

There can be no true, lasting anointing until the death of self is experientially lived out in Christ. This is the place where yokes of bondage become broken by anything we say. I do not want to simply speak "high-tech, fleshly controlled" words that sound super-spiritual, yet result in nothing more than an expression of human wisdom. I want to die out completely to all *self*-will.

In the same spirit as expressed by the late Kathryn Kuhlman, I want to know the place, the hour, the moment where Kim Wetteland died — leaving only Christ to remain. I want to become so much like Jesus on the inside that anything I speak will carry great power and lasting authority on the outside.

This kind of authority is available for all, but a price must be paid to receive it. The question I would like to leave with you is this: Are *you* willing to pay that price?

5

A Mystery Hidden in Christ

God's will is that every Christian be conformed into the image of His Son, Jesus Christ. As mentioned in chapter 2, the Greek word for *image* is *eikon*, which means "exact likeness, resemblance, or representation.

For whom he did foreknow, he also did predestinate to be conformed to the image of his Son . . . .

Romans 8:29

You are not to be a "little bit" like Jesus; you are to be exactly like Him. This is what you were predestinated for since before the foundation of the world: To be like Jesus! To experience His strength! To live in His power! Yet, how can this be? In Colossians, we find this is a mystery hidden away in Christ.

Even the mystery which hath been hid from ages and from generations, but now is made manifest to his saints:

To whom God would make known what is the riches of the glory of this mystery among the Gentiles; which is Christ in you, the hope of glory.

Colossians 1:26,27

Please notice that transformation into the exact image and likeness of Jesus is not a mystery that is hidden away in works, personal striving, a special teaching, or the efforts of the flesh. No! The secret of becoming like Christ is to join yourself to Christ. This is done through intimate, daily fellowship with Him — worship, prayer, and time spent in the study of His Word.

As 1 Corinthians 6:7 says, when you consistently join yourself to Jesus, you are *one spirit* with Him. His likeness is your likeness. Your likeness is His likeness. There is no difference. You and Jesus are exactly alike.

I am so thankful to be married to my wife, Simone, a lovely woman who has given me four beautiful children: Alicia, Audrey, Raquel, and Tamra.

Recently, I was sitting on the bed with Alicia, Raquel, and Audrey. We were having our nighttime Bible study and saying goodnight-prayers. The topic of discussion was how to become like Jesus. We joined hands, prayed, and read Romans 8:29.

The very simple terms in that verse were easy for my girls to understand.

I said, "Now, girls, this scripture means that Father God wants each one of *you* to be just like Jesus."

Our girls get excited during Bible study. With big smiles and loud voices, they all yelled "Yeah!"

A good "rule of thumb" to follow for teaching small children is repetition. So I asked them over and over who God wanted them to be like.

At the top of their lungs, they shouted, "Jesus! Jesus! Jesus!"

Then, in a simple and forthright manner, I began to tell my girls that trying to *act* like Jesus will never make us *be* like Him. Sometimes I think we spend too much time trying to make children do what is right, and little — if any — time introducing them to Jesus as a Person. Even children, when guided daily into the presence of Christ, will begin to change and bring forth the Holy Spirit's fruit.

We see this happen over and over in our Super-Church Program. A child meets Jesus and is born again, receives the baptism of the Holy Spirit, and begins to change.

> **And they kept bringing young children to Him that He might touch them, and the disciples were reproving them** [for it].

> **But when Jesus saw** [it]**, He was indignant and pained and said to them, Allow the children to come to Me — do not forbid or prevent or hinder them — for to such belongs the kingdom of God.**
> **Mark 10:13,14 AMP**

As a parent, you have a responsibility to take your child into the presence of Christ on a daily basis. Teach your child by example to pray, praise, and worship the Almighty Living God. By doing this, you will be a part of helping your child become transformed into the exact image and likeness of Christ. Jesus said the Kingdom of God belongs to children, as well as adults: . . . **for to such belongs the Kingdom of God** (Mark 10:14 AMP).

Romans 14:17 tells us that the Kingdom of God is righteousness, peace, and joy in the Holy Spirit, that the Kingdom is not rules and regulations. Righteousness, peace, and joy are fruit. Jesus is telling us that the fruit of the Spirit is also for children. As we bring our children into the presence of Christ, they will bring forth fruit. They will change. The responsibility of teaching our children to spend time with God so that this transformation process may take place, however, lies solely with us as parents.

As we continued our Bible study, I read another scripture.

> **Come close to God and He will come close to you . . . .**
> **James 4:8 AMP**

Again in very simple terms, I said, "Girls, this verse means that if we lift our hands way up toward the sky to God and say, 'Jesus, I love you,' God will get real close to us and make us like Jesus."

Over and over, I shared this truth, then asked them, "How do you get to be like Jesus?"

Each raised her little hands high in the air with a grin on her face as wide as the Grand Canyon, and shouted, "Jesus, I love You! Jesus, I love You! Jesus, I love You!" Sometimes my oldest daughter, Alicia, surprises me. As Raquel and Audrey continued joyfully shouting "Jesus, I love You," Alicia began to sing a Spirit-inspired love song to Christ in her own words.

Through this simple process of bringing our children into the presence of Christ daily, Simone and I have watched them change **from glory to glory, even as by the Spirit of the Lord** (2 Cor. 3:18).

Becoming Like Jesus Is Not Hard

Although this illustration is simple, I think you get my point. Becoming like Jesus is not difficult. A willing heart is all that is required. Without Christ, we can do nothing. We cannot conform ourselves into His image. It is a joint effort. Our efforts mean coming into His presence and yielding to Him; His effort is to work in our inward beings by the Holy Spirit to conform us into the exact likeness of Himself.

We do not see this transformation process depicted anywhere more clearly than in the transfiguration of Christ as recorded in Luke.

> **And it came to pass about an eight days after these sayings, he took Peter and John and James, and went up into a mountain *to pray.***
>
> **And as he *prayed*, the fashion of his countenance was altered, and his raiment was white and glistering.**
> **Luke 9:28,29**

Jesus took Peter, John, and James up into a mountain and began to pray. As He prayed, something very powerful took place. His countenance was altered. While sitting in the presence of the Father, His flesh changed. His outward appearance changed. Even the clothes He wore began to shine with the glory of God's majesty. Please notice these things took place while Jesus was praying. *The place of prayer is the place of change.* In the place of prayer, we are fashioned into the exact image and likeness of Christ. The place of prayer is where self-will and flesh are crucified.

> **. . . But if ye through the *Spirit* do mortify the deeds of the body, ye shall live.**
>
> **Romans 8:13**

Do you want to change? Go to the place of prayer. In the presence of the Holy Spirit, your human, fleshly will cannot survive. For this reason, many refuse to pray with any regularity. In their hearts, they know the end of self-directed ambitions are inevitable, so they do not pray. Many are those who go to church, teach Sunday school, sing in the choir, and even preach. But few are those who silently commune with the Living God in prayer until a true change is birthed by that which only the Holy Spirit can do.

The question really is not, "How can we become fashioned into the glorious image of Jesus Christ?" Deep within the inward man, every Christian knows this happens as we consistently meet Jesus in the place of prayer. The real questions are, "*Who* will do this? Who will take up his cross and follow Jesus? Who will lay down personal plans, goals, and pursuits to spend time alone with Christ?"

Some months ago, Audrey was very ill. As much as I desired to pray for her, I had a "check" in my spirit to wait. I knew I had to get alone with Jesus first. Sometimes, we pray too quickly for things, not finding the heart of God in the matter. Flesh can be an imitator of spiritual things but will never produce the same results.

In the presence of Jesus, there is life, peace, and power. If we would learn to spend time alone with Christ before we pray for something, the results would be powerful and long-lasting. While kneeling to pray, I could sense the glory of God begin to cover me. I prayed like this:

"Jesus, while I'm in Your presence, make me to be just a little more like You. Raise me up to a new level of glory. Oh, God, wash all my self-will away by Your Spirit. Allow Christ only to remain."

Over and over I prayed in this fashion. Then I prayed in other tongues. Praying in tongues brings change also.

> **But ye, beloved, building up yourselves on your most holy faith, praying in the Holy Ghost,**
>
> **Keep yourselves in the love of God, looking for the mercy of our Lord Jesus Christ unto eternal life.**
>
> **Jude 20,21**

To pray in the Spirit, or in other tongues, is to literally abide in the presence of God. This brings change and results in the fruit of the Spirit being vividly displayed in your life. As you pray in tongues, the Spirit of Life Himself flows through your spirit, washes across your soul, and sinks deep within every cell of your physical body. Your inward man becomes changed.

On the inside, you are fashioned into the exact likeness and glorious image of Jesus. Your mind, will, and emotions will be renewed with spiritual power, and your physical body will become energized with divine health. Prayer brings you into the presence of God. You cannot sit in the presence of a holy God for more than a few moments without experiencing the blessing of His great covenant.

For more than a half-hour, I continued to pray in this fashion:

"God, change me. Transform me just a little more into the glorious image of Jesus."

Then I would pray in other tongues. Finally, I knew it was time to pray for Audrey. God's glory was upon me. The fashion of my countenance had changed. My flesh had lost all of its control. I could sense Jesus oozing out of my spirit with great power.

When I laid my hands on Audrey, the glory fell.

"You foul, hellish disease, with the lightnings of the Spirit and the name of Jesus, I drive you out of my little girl," I shouted.

Instantly, Audrey stopped coughing, the fever left, and she slept peacefully until the next morning. As the dawn broke, Audrey was up and as chipper as ever. There was no sign that she had been sick the night before. She was completely well.

I learned a great lesson from this experience. If you are faithful to spend time in God's presence so He can fashion you into the likeness of Christ on the inside, your words will manifest great power and lasting authority on the outside.

6

Mantles of Extraordinary Power

The ministry of the great Old Testament prophet Elijah had come to a close. On his final historic journey, Elijah stopped in the cities of Gilgal, Bethel, and Jericho. Elisha, a student in the ministry under the instruction of Elijah, followed tenaciously alongside the great man of God. After many days of strenuous travel, they reached their destination — the Jordan River.

And Elijah took his mantle, and wrapped it together, and smote the waters, and they were divided hither and thither, so that they two went over on dry ground.

And it came to pass, when they were gone over, that Elijah said unto Elisha, ask what I shall do for thee, before I be taken away from thee. And Elisha said, I pray thee, let a double portion of thy spirit be upon me.

2 Kings 2:9

The time for Elijah to make his great departure had come. The chariots of fire were waiting. Elisha had asked for a hard thing — a double portion of the anointing carried by Elijah. A moment of silence echoed through the great Jordan Valley, as the sons of the prophets watched nearby. The answer then came:

. . . If thou see me when I am taken from thee, it shall be so unto thee; but if not, it shall not be so.

2 Kings 2:10

Elijah was saying, "Elisha, you must be in the Spirit when I leave. You cannot be ruled by your fleshly passions.

47

You must be willing to experience a total crucifixion of your flesh. If you fulfill this condition, you will be able to see with the eyes of your inward man. You will peer into the Spirit realm and view my departure. If you can walk this close with God, a double portion of my anointing shall be yours. If you cannot, you will never have it.''

Elijah and Elisha continued on their journey. The account recorded in 2 Kings does not tell us how long, how far, or how many more days they traveled.

> **And it came to pass, as they still went on, and talked, that, behold, there appeared a chariot of fire, and horses of fire, and parted them both asunder; and Elijah went up by a whirlwind into heaven.**
>
> **And Elisha saw it, and he cried, my Father, my Father, the chariot of Israel, and the horseman thereof . . . .**
>
> **2 Kings 2:11,12**

Elisha fulfilled the condition given to him by Elijah. He was willing to pay the price of dying out to self. As a result, he received a mantle of extraordinary power.

Dr. Lester Sumrall of South Bend, Indiana, is a man who used to visit the late great British evangelist Smith Wigglesworth and who preached with him on many occasions. His personal accounts of the way Wigglesworth ministered to the sick are very interesting. Here is one of those stories:

> In the same church where I was preaching, the great Glad Tidings Tabernacle, which seated more than 3,000 people at that time, Wigglesworth was preaching in a Sunday afternoon healing service. They brought people from hospitals, in wheelchairs, portable hospital beds, etc. for Smith Wigglesworth to pray for them. From one of the local hospitals, a doctor brought a very severe cancer case. Actually, he hadn't wanted to bring him, because the man was so near death.

I went over and sat beside his little hospital bed on the platform, and here came Smith Wigglesworth, who was a bit gruff, down the line, praying for the people.

The way he would ask you what was wrong with you was this: "What's up?"

In his part of England, that was a familiar way of speaking. "What's up?" was the same as saying, "What ails you? What is wrong with you?"

He got to this cancer patient who was stretched out on the bed, wearing a little hospital gown that had no buttons up the back. The doctor was sitting there with his stethoscope in his ears, listening to the man's heartbeat and letting everyone know the man was very near death. When Wigglesworth said, "What's up?", the doctor replied, "He is dying of cancer."

Wigglesworth asked, "Where is it?"

The doctor said, "In his stomach."

And Smith Wigglesworth, probably the most unusual person I have ever met in my life, wound up his arm and with his fist hit him where the cancer was, right in the stomach! The man's hands fell off the bed, and the doctor screamed, "He's dead! He's dead!"

Then the doctor looked up and said, "You killed him! You killed him! The family will sue you. You killed him."

Wigglesworth wasn't upset one bit. He said, "He's 'ealed." (That's the way he'd say, "He's healed;" he didn't pronounce "h's.") He said, "He's 'ealed," and he didn't stop. He just went on down the line, praying.

About ten minutes later, here came the man! He'd gotten up off the hospital bed, moved the doctor to one side, and begun to walk in that funny little hospital gown that was open in the back. Here he was, following

Smith Wigglesworth, with his hands up in the air, praising God.

He said, "I have no pain. I feel wonderful inside. I have energy I have not had for I don't know how long."

This sort of thing was so normal with him (Smith Wigglesworth), he said, "Well, just thank God for it," and went on praying for people. (Liardon, Roberts, edit. "Unpublished Sermons of Smith Wigglesworth," *Cry of the Spirit* (Tulsa: Harrison House Publishing, 1989), pp. 8,9.)

Mantles Await Those Who Pay the Price

History records heroes of faith, who for an eternal testimony demonstrated great feats of supernatural power as an example for us to follow. God is no respecter of persons. For those willing to yield to the Holy Spirit's deeper purgings and die to self, there awaits great mantles of extraordinary power. The mighty miracles that took place through men such as Smith Wigglesworth can also happen through you!

As I mentioned in chapter 5, Jesus took Peter, John, and James up into a mountain and began to pray. (Luke 9:28-36.) Verse 29 says His countenance was altered. He changed. Something else happened when Jesus prayed that I want you to particularly notice. Moses and Elijah appeared. These two were Old Testament prophets anointed with mantles of extraordinary ability and power. They talked to Jesus about His coming crucifixion in Jerusalem.

After their conversation, Peter, John, and James awoke. They had been asleep and had not heard a word that was said. In a complete state of shock, Peter thanked Jesus for the honor of being invited to this great event and wanted to build three tabernacles. Surely Peter must have thought Jesus was setting up His earthly Kingdom.

Suddenly, a cloud of glory from heaven overshadowed all of them. The disciples were in great fear as a voice came out of the cloud saying, **This is my beloved Son: hear him** (Luke 9:35).

Certainly the disciples thought they had received the message correctly. Jesus was setting up His Kingdom. Right? The three were taken up into the mountain where Jesus began to pray and was transfigured before them. Moses and Elijah appeared and talked to Him in detail, at which the disciples awoke only to be overcome by the holy presence of God and by His voice.

But what did God really want these three fishermen to hear?

There is an old saying that is very true: Actions speak louder than words. The fact that two Old Testament prophets, who had been anointed with mantles of great, extraordinary power, appeared on the scene while Jesus prayed and was transfigured is no accident. Jesus was showing the three disciples how to receive these mantles.

Tucked away in the presence of Jesus lie mantles of extraordinary power for those who dare to go and receive them. These mantles go far beyond authority over demons, diseases, and disasters. These mantles have authority and power to break the control of nature itself.

How are they received? Only as we stand in His presence, for in God's presence, no flesh can stand. Pride, arrogancy, and self-directed ambitions all die, swallowed up by the life of Jesus. This is a painful process. The inward and emotional pain of experiencing the death of self is, at times, almost unbearable.

Forasmuch then as Christ hath suffered for us in the flesh, arm yourselves likewise with the same mind: for he that hath suffered in the flesh hath ceased from sin.

1 Peter 4:1

This is why Christ agonized and sweat as it were great drops of blood. Yet He persisted, crying out, "Not my will, but thine be done." Alone in the presence of God, the death of self finds its completion as Christ fully becomes imaged within the inward man. We have changed. No longer are we the same. As John the Baptist said: **He must increase, but I must decrease** (John 3:30).

Through this transformation comes the impartation of an anointing containing mantles of great and extraordinary power. For as you are fashioned into the exact image and likeness of Jesus on the inside, anything you say or do will demonstrate great, supernatural power and authority on the outside.

Several years ago, I went out to share the Gospel with a street-witnessing team in Tulsa. We met at 4:30 p.m. to pray. For hours, we labored in earnest prayer for the souls of men. With strong cries and groanings of the Spirit, we pulled down many strongholds. Then we entered into a time of praise and worship.

A delightful ecstasy of joy filled the atmosphere of that room. Then the glory fell, followed by tongues, interpretation, and great prophetic words of victory. We had touched the heart of God and everyone knew it. The time now was 8 p.m. It was time to go forth. While departing, each of us left with a knowing on the inside that something mighty was going to take place that evening.

Our steps were surely guided by the Lord as we made our way to a hangout where international students frequently gathered. John and Tim were the first to arrive. As I met with them later, they were talking with two students from Lebanon.

"Hey, Kim! Come and meet two new friends," John called excitedly. "These guys are Christian Muslims!"

Concerned, I asked, "Christian Muslims?" That sounded like a contradiction to me. After thoroughly questioning the two students, John and Tim realized they had "the wool pulled over their eyes." Those Muslim boys believed Jesus was a good man, a prophet, and a teacher, but they absolutely denied His Lordship and Deity.

"Jesus is not God! No! He was only a good man," they said with boldness.

Suddenly, to my right, a group of hecklers began to gather. They laughed, jeered, scorned, and mocked us for publicly sharing Christ with others. A holy boldness quickly arose within me that to this day I cannot describe. With an authority I did not even realize existed, I turned toward that group of hecklers and said, "Freeze!"

Before my very eyes, and before the eyes of John, Tim, and about forty witnesses, those hecklers immediately froze motionless, unable to move!

"You say Jesus is not God, and you don't know Him? Well, now, you are about to meet Him as the power of the Holy Spirit, whom you also deny, touches you from on high!"

As I waved my arm, a tangible manifestation of the Holy Spirit's presence hit the two Muslims, lifted them completely off their feet, and carried them against a wall about two feet behind them.

When they hit the wall, the group of hecklers who had been frozen in a motionless state, thawed out. They all ran off together. I wish I could say each of them received Jesus in his heart, but I cannot. The crowd of onlookers, however, talked with us one by one. Many of them were born again and baptized in the Holy Spirit that evening. Those who were sick or in need of deliverance were healed.

I believe we have reached the day that men and women of God will again arise with great mantles of extraordinary ability and power. We shall see it! Together, we shall watch the world stand in wonder at the Almighty glory of God.

Jesus said that we were to do His works, only greater. (John 14:12.)

In today's society, people are hurting as never before. There are cripples who need to walk and broken hearts that need mending. There are blind eyes yet to be opened and thousands crying out for someone to bring them the genuine life-changing power of Jesus Christ.

There are many mantles of great, extraordinary ability and power waiting to be received so hurting people might be set free through the grace and love of Jesus Christ. The question again is: Who will pay the price to receive these mantles?

About the Author

At the age of fifteen, Kim Wetteland was raised off his death bed and healed of a serious heart ailment. He is currently senior pastor of Victory Christian Center in Des Moines, Iowa, and serves as an international director for Dr. Lester Sumrall's Feed the Hungry Program.

The focal point of Kim's ministry centers around Romans 8:29:

> **For whom he did foreknow, he also did predestinate to be conformed to the image of his Son . . . .**

Kim boldly declares to his generation the necessity of yielding to the Holy Spirit's work of transforming the believer into the image of Jesus Christ and of bearing a genuine Christ-likeness as a foundation for carrying a true, lasting anointing.

Kim and his lovely wife, Simone, are the proud parents of four beautiful daughters: Alicia, Raquel Ann, Audrey Joy, and Tamra. In addition to *Christ in You: A Revelation of God's Power*, he is the author of *Nation Changers*.

To invite Kim Wetteland to minister in your area,
please write:

Kim Wetteland Ministries
P.O. Box 7652
Des Moines, Iowa 50322

Or call: (515) 276-1763

Additional copies of this book are available
from your local bookstore or from:

Harrison House
P. O. Box 35035
Tulsa, Oklahoma 74153

In Canada contact:

Word Alive
P. O. Box 284
Niverville, Manitoba
CANADA ROA 1 EO

For international sales in Europe contact:

Harrison House Europe
Belruptstrasse 42 A
A — 6900 Bregenz
AUSTRIA

The Harrison House Vision

Proclaiming the truth and power
Of the Gospel of Jesus Christ
With excellence;

Challenging Christians to
Live victoriously,
Grow spiritually,
Know God intimately.